Brands We Know

Hershey's

By Sara Green

Bellwether Media • Minneapolis, MN

Jump into the cockpit and take flight with Pilot books. Your journey will take you on high-energy adventures as you learn about all that is wild, weird, fascinating, and fun!

This edition first published in 2015 by Bellwether Media, Inc.

No part of this publication may be reproduced in whole or in part without written permission of the publisher.
For information regarding permission, write to Bellwether Media, Inc.,
Attention: Permissions Department,
5357 Penn Avenue South, Minneapolis, MN 55419.

Library of Congress Cataloging-in-Publication Data

Green, Sara, 1964-
  Hershey's / by Sara Green.
    pages cm. -- (Pilot: Brands We Know)
  Includes bibliographical references and index.
  Summary: "Engaging images accompany information about the
Hershey Company. The combination of high-interest subject matter
and narrative text is intended for students in grades 3 through 7"--
Provided by publisher.
  Audience: 7-12.
  Audience: Grades 3-7.
  ISBN 978-1-62617-206-7 (hardcover : alk. paper)
  1. Hershey Foods Corporation--History--Juvenile literature. 2.
Hershey, Milton Snavely, 1857-1945--Juvenile literature. 3. Chocolate
industry--United States--History--Juvenile literature. 4. Hershey (Pa.)-
-Juvenile literature. I. Title.
  HD9200.U54H477 2015
  338.7'6641530973--dc23
                    2014036503

Printed in the United States of America, North Mankato, MN.

Table of Contents

What Is Hershey's?

Chocolate is a favorite treat enjoyed by people around the world. This delicious food can be served in many ways. People like to eat chocolate candy bars and chocolate chip cookies. They pour chocolate syrup on ice cream and drink it in milk. Hot chocolate warms people on cold winter days. Much of this chocolate comes from The Hershey Company, founded by Milton S. Hershey in 1894.

The Hershey Company is one of the largest **manufacturers** of chocolate in the world. It was originally named the Hershey Chocolate Company. However, the company of today makes more than just chocolate. It also makes hard candy, gum, mints, and peanut butter. The Hershey Company **exports** products to 90 countries. This makes Hershey's one of the most popular **brands** on Earth. In 2013, the company made more than $7 billion in sales!

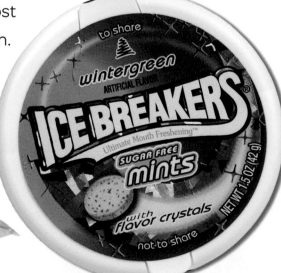

By the Numbers

about
13,000
employees

$19.6 million
in sales each day

about
80 million
Hershey's Kisses
produced per day

**300,000 to
350,000**
gallons (1.1 million to
1.3 million liters) of fresh milk
used in the West Hershey
factory per day

1 million
miles (1.6 million kilometers)
of Twizzlers Twists
produced each year

nearly
250 million
Hershey's Bars sold in 2012

Milton S. Hershey

Milton S. Hershey was born in Derry Township, Pennsylvania, in 1857. At age 14, he started work as an **apprentice** at a candy shop in Lancaster, Pennsylvania. Milton enjoyed this job. He became a highly skilled candymaker. In 1876, Milton opened his own taffy shop. However, sales were slow. After six years, the shop closed. He then moved to Denver, Colorado, where he learned how to make caramel candy.

Milton S. Hershey

In 1886, Milton returned to Pennsylvania. That year he opened the Lancaster Caramel Company. He wanted to make the best caramel candy in the world. Milton only used fresh milk to make caramels. This gave them a creamy taste. It also helped them stay fresh longer than other caramels. An English businessman was impressed when he tasted Milton's candy. He placed a large order of caramels to be shipped to England. The money from this order helped the caramel company grow quickly. Milton's company was a success!

Lancaster Caramel Company

The Hershey Chocolate Company

In 1893, Milton attended a fair in Chicago, Illinois. There, he saw equipment that made chocolate. It fascinated him so much that he bought it. In 1894, Milton launched the Hershey Chocolate Company. The company's main purpose was to make chocolate to coat the Lancaster caramels. Baking chocolate and cocoa were other products. Milton also made chocolate candy in shapes such as bicycles and lobsters.

Cuban Sugar

In 1916, Milton bought his first sugar mill in Cuba. There, he started making sugar for Hershey's chocolate. He also built a town for the workers and a railroad to transport them and the sugar. Milton's Cuban properties were sold in 1946.

At that time, only the Swiss knew how to make milk chocolate. It was very expensive and only wealthy people could afford it. Milton had a goal.

He wanted to make delicious, affordable milk chocolate. For years, he tried different methods. No recipe was quite right. Finally, in 1899, Milton created a recipe that satisfied him. He used it to make America's first milk chocolate candy bar. Milton called it the Hershey's Bar. It sold for only a nickel. Soon, the Hershey's Bar became one of the world's best-selling chocolate bars.

A Town Called Hershey

The success of the milk chocolate bar forced Milton to make a decision. He did not have time to make both caramels and chocolate. Milton decided his future was in chocolate. So in 1900, Milton sold the Lancaster Caramel Company for $1 million. He used this money to expand the chocolate company.

The Hershey Chocolate Company grew rapidly. Soon, Milton needed more space. In 1903, Milton began building a larger factory near his hometown of Derry Township. He also hired more workers. They needed a place to live with their families. Milton decided to build them a town near the factory. It was named Hershey. The new town had houses, churches, schools, and parks. Later, it also had swimming pools and a zoo. Milton hoped to attract **tourists** to the town. He even included postcards of Hershey in his

chocolate bars. His efforts paid off. Thousands of visitors arrived to see the town and tour the chocolate factory.

Hersheypark

Hersheypark is an amusement park in Hershey, Pennsylvania. It has more than 60 rides, including 12 roller coasters. More than 3 million people visit the park each year.

More Than a Chocolate Bar

As Hershey, Pennsylvania grew, the company started making new products. In 1907, it introduced the Kiss. This bite of milk chocolate came in a teardrop shape. Each small candy was wrapped in silver foil by hand. In 1921, the Hershey Chocolate Company added a short flag to the wrapping. The flag identified the candy as a Hershey's Kiss.

A Kiss for Everyone!
Hershey's Kisses come in a variety of flavors. Favorites include milk chocolate, dark chocolate, caramel, and with almonds.

Every day deserves a Kiss
2010s tagline

Hershey's
Miniatures

Hershey's
Syrup

The Hershey's Bar and Kisses were huge sellers. By 1921, the Hershey Chocolate Company was making $20 million in yearly sales. Still the company continued to add new products. In 1925, Hershey's introduced a chocolate bar with peanuts called the Mr. Goodbar. In 1926, Hershey's began making chocolate syrup. People used it to top ice cream. They also mixed it with milk and soda to make chocolate drinks. In 1928, chocolate chips were introduced. Another popular chocolate bar, Krackel, **debuted** in 1938. Hershey's Miniatures appeared the next year. People loved these small versions of Hershey's candy bars!

Other kinds of candy soon followed. During World War II, the company made Field **Ration** D Bars. These candy bars were made for troops fighting in the war. They had extra **vitamins** and did not melt. Hershey's made more than three billion ration bars for the soldiers.

In 1963, the chocolate company bought the H.B. Reese Candy Company. Its most popular candy was the Peanut Butter Cup. Hershey's had always made the chocolate coating for the cups. Now it would also be responsible for making and **marketing** the candy. Reese's Peanut Butter Cups would become one of the

Field Ration D Bar

most popular candy brands of all time.

Today, Hershey's also makes other products. Some of the most popular are Jolly Ranchers and Twizzlers. Hershey's Syrup now comes in several flavors, including strawberry and caramel. Hershey's also owns an **organic** chocolate bar brand called Dagoba. With so many choices, people may not be able to decide which Hershey's product is their favorite!

Two great tastes that taste great together

1970s-1980s tagline for Reese's Peanut Butter Cups

Popular Hershey's Products

By Year Added to Company

Hershey's Milk Chocolate Bar 1900

Hershey's Kisses 1907

Mr. Goodbar 1925

Hershey's Syrup 1926

Krackel Bar 1938

Hershey's Miniatures 1939

Reese's Peanut Butter Cups 1963

Hershey's Special Dark Bar 1971

Twizzlers 1977

York Peppermint Pattie 1988

Symphony Bar 1989

Cookies 'n' Creme Bar 1994

Jolly Ranchers 1996

Bubble Yum 2000

Hershey's Helping Hand

The Hershey Company has a long history of helping people. In 1909, Milton Hershey and his wife, Catherine, started a school in Hershey, Pennsylvania, for **orphaned** boys. It was called the Hershey **Industrial** School. The first class had ten students. Catherine died a few years after the school opened. After her death, Milton donated $60 million in land and money to the school. This was his entire fortune. Milton stayed involved with the school until he died in 1945.

Milton and Catherine Hershey

Hershey Industrial School

Milton Hershey School

In 1951, the name of the school changed. It became the Milton Hershey School. Today, about 2,000 boys and girls attend the school every year. All students come from **low-income** families. The school provides them with a free education from preschool through grade twelve. Students live on campus, where they receive free meals and medical care. They can participate in sports, choir, theater, and many other activities. Most students attend college after they graduate.

Milton's **tradition** of giving is honored in other ways, too. The Hershey Company participates in many programs that help people. One of these is called Project Peanut Butter. This program uses peanuts to make **nutritious** food for hungry children in Africa. The food helps the children grow up strong and healthy. Project Peanut Butter uses peanuts grown in the country where the food is distributed. This helps that

country's **economy**. Workers also teach local farmers **efficient** methods for planting and harvesting peanuts.

The Hershey Company also aims to sell chocolate that comes from **sustainable** sources. Chocolate is made from cocoa beans. This crop is grown in **tropical** places around the world. Most of Hershey's chocolate comes from cocoa beans grown in Africa. There, The Hershey Company is helping teach farmers how to grow cocoa beans in ways that keep the soil healthy. This knowledge helps farmers grow more crops and protect the environment at the same time. Through chocolate and actions, Hershey's brings goodness to the world.

Hershey's Timeline

1857
Milton S. Hershey is born in Pennsylvania on September 13

1906
The town is officially named Hershey

1909
Milton and his wife, Catherine, open the Hershey Industrial School

1900
The Hershey Chocolate Company introduces the Hershey's Bar

1928
The first Reese's Peanut Butter Cup is made with Hershey's chocolate

1886
Milton starts the Lancaster Caramel Company

1871
Milton starts work as a candymaker's apprentice in Lancaster, Pennsylvania

1921
Kisses are wrapped by machine and the flag is added to the wrapping

1903
Milton begins construction on the Hershey Factory and a town in Derry Township, Pennsylvania

1894
Milton starts the Hershey Chocolate Company

1907
Hersheypark opens

2005
The company name changes to
The Hershey Company

1962
Kisses are wrapped in
colors other than silver for
the first time

1945
Milton passes away in
Hershey, Pennsylvania,
on October 13

2014
Hershey's changes
its logo

2004
Hershey's net sales
reach $4.4 billion

Glossary

apprentice—a person who works for a more skilled person in order to learn a trade

brands—categories of products all made by the same company

debuted—was introduced for the first time

economy—the wealth and resources of a country

efficient—producing in a way that does not waste resources

exports—sends products to other countries

industrial—relating to factories

low-income—not making much money

manufacturers—companies that make items for people to use

marketing—promoting and selling a product

nutritious—healthy

organic—made without artificial chemicals

orphaned—when both parents have died

ration—a particular amount of food given for one day; soldiers receive food rations while on duty to make sure there is enough food for everyone.

sustainable—able to be used without being completely used up or destroyed

tourists—people who travel to visit another place

tradition—a custom, belief, or way of life that has been handed down from one generation to the next

tropical—having a hot, wet climate

vitamins—natural substances found in food that help the body stay healthy

To Learn More

AT THE LIBRARY

Buckley, James, Jr. *Who Was Milton Hershey?* New York, N.Y.: Grosset & Dunlap, 2013.

Eboch, M.M. *Milton Hershey: Young Chocolatier*. New York, N.Y.: Aladdin Paperbacks, 2008.

Love, Ann, and Jane Drake. *Sweet! The Delicious Story of Candy*. New York, N.Y.: Tundra Books of Northern New York, 2007.

ON THE WEB

Learning more about Hershey's is as easy as 1, 2, 3.

1. Go to www.factsurfer.com.

2. Enter "Hershey's" into the search box.

3. Click the "Surf" button and you will see a list of related web sites.

With factsurfer.com, finding more information is just a click away.

Index